TANGERINE SUN

POEMS BY
SEPPO ODELL

ALPHAGLYPH PUBLICATIONS
VANCOUVER BC CANADA

Tangerine Sun © Seppo Odell 2018

ISBN: 978-1-988368-01-6
Cover Art by Marty Holladay (photography by Ashley Connolly)

AlphaGlyph Publications, Vancouver, Canada
www.odell.shamcher.com

Toward the One

Lake

a squashed tangerine sun
squints
bittersweet,
lifting clean
green
lake water to the ethers,
drawing sprites to the fine spray.
at the bottom
sleep-maidens pull threads
unraveling childhood knots
from the colorless carpet of impressions,
making smooth
gray grooved ridges
on the surface of the brain.
tickling
first time laughter.

GOODNESS

under the lifted veils
that wave over the gray earth winds
children are killing themselves
quietly.
when they die they are unknown,
usually alone
as death approaches they sleep into the overdose,
calming the getting more.
these souls journey off planet, finishing their work
leaving a signature of fierce light.
their pattern of a twisting life finally untangled
there are loudmouths on tv
reaching for auto sales and votes,
"in the american style"
of yelling.

there are cars going by with driversmind stirring
sending out mental stuff
causing
thinking something is going on in other driversminds
causing rage
but there really is nothing going on

Goodness abounds
above karma and dharma on the spiritual measuring scale.
no one understands karma and dharma

Seppo Odell

Goodness pervades everything
is in everything!
junkies
loudmouths
drivers
cars.

SAMSARA

you come in holy rags muttering teachings,
complaining about the miso soup,
telling me about your golden pooja table
telling me how to toe the spiritual line,
pointing with a long fingernail.

you are the mission bishop in the amazon with your priest army,
columbus whispers in your ear, "but, they are savages."
the beautiful painted faces smile,
"we are humans."
you use Jesus' sweetness
like it were table salt
to get their gold.

i hear clicking prayer beads,
chanting mantra,
everyone looks so special,
the followers
that pay the bills.

how does this happen?
pluto in leo?
narcissist parents?
tell your chelas to go home
leave them alone!

no one carried you off to bed
Tucked you in, kissed you good night.

your outer petals have dried up
brittle
let them fall
juicy ones are waiting for you to flower
mingle your perfume with the perfume of all beings.

Seppo Odell

THE BAR

the bar is love itself
voices thrown to voices with lies that grin.
a teen man drinks his first pint
elders circle glasses
the *shebeen* stories begin a long night.

children brighten
the adults drinking
their feelings release
making way for a deeper joy.

Brooklyn girls group
in a safe booth
to meet a guy
make *boxty* and babies

old songs are sung
poems wrung
pains from the past rise up
into a false heaven
the capacity for sorrow
contained by the pub roof.

in the corner an old woman
from Sky Road
with a jug of punch
smiles at all who smile,
exhausting the crimes of the church,
healing the marks left on her skin.

Past Lives

déjà vu is a pulled trigger
without a bullet.
just breeze holding air
making the sky absent,
a hole
between
vacant moments
like
that soft faraway sound of a familiar screen door
slamming
somewhere out back

I rose above the steel sea
still hearing
droning
Lancasters
fly their sortie to the Rhineland
now
smaller
distant
humming
away into the black and white.
I remember the pause
the metal click of a luger
the shock
the slug in the back
in a damp cell in Anschluss Austria.

repeating the rapid run through the heavens
another Jew untying their shoes
another nervous end
starting

another relentless life
in New York City

Seppo Odell

a sleeveless university woman,
both coarse and soft.
an activist
writing about the new Nazis:
selling war
selling fear insurance,
jailing anyone colored
in the supersized ghetto
where America does not live long on chips n' beer.

CRISIS

By the time you look up
startled by your smart phone emanations
suddenly aware of the rushing minutes
unsure
unaware that no one called you.

You feel the heat of ripened middle age:
the future fears
the worries of accomplishment
the money tightening.

The god of reason and logic cannot help you out of your
crisis,
or release you from the concentration camp of thinking.

Turn off the phone heroin.
be still
deeply see and feel
how stiff and brittle you have become
like dry twigs that snap.

The truth is that you were born soft, supple.
wearing a mind and body
like a jewel necklace surrounding your soul
a warm glow of warm gold light
the delight of knowing
with certainty
you have a purpose to be here.

Seppo Odell

A Step Towards Perfection

as the cosmos dances
we sway on the front porch playing dominoes.
countless star beings hold their breath for your next move!
you pause and search for sea shells on another shore
while placing a tile on the board
holding the ocean
as your jewel.

your love is delicate, as you are tender,
a treasure to me.

i am falling in your folding spaces
dressed in the feminine mystery
beyond
the order that events appear to take
without age
without imperfection.

Summer Sweat

working men are drinking after work
they were in the war
their sameness to each other
is somewhere way back in their memory,
bringing momentary joy
of belonging
living as a living tribe,
there is no sense of "my country"
there is no *nation*
just a distant myth.

be at ease in your life
you are a part
that fits
you share parts of yourself with others.
cells from one
are in another
over and over again
in one puzzle,
clean like a canyon made by rain.

Seppo Odell

A Hole in the Heart

Black Elk returned to camp,
after his first time with the whites,
he spoke at council,
"the few have more than the rest,
they hold this pain tightly.
this is a mental disorder
that disturbs their community,
causing anger and fear.

But they are the same as we
they walk upon on the same mother
under the same sky, we should try to get along with them."
pausing he thought to himself,
"they will eventually want to destroy us."

100 years have passed,
the wound of wounded knee has not healed,
the few still have more than the rest and do not share.
this hole in the heart cannot be filled
by going to the mall
consuming more and then more numbness.

The tracks left in the snow by the bear
are not the bear
so you are not
but a play of hide and seek
until eventually you stop
and discover who you are.

Living Without a Menu

ageing is free
like skin breathing
free to behave
calmly
or not behave.
free to fake it
to be still,
watching
stillness itself
while ordering
in this noisy bar
static cracking
breaking thoughts.

there is no special face
but all faces appear
as mirrors of love
the waitress
unclothed
from thoughts
asks
"gravy on the fries, hun?"

Seppo Odell

THE SERIOUS JOY OF FORGIVENESS

There were more cops than needed
for just one unarmed boy
turns out he *was* armed
with his black skin.
he knew to keep his hands up
like mama said, "hands up when they come for you"
but it didn't matter
they fired anyway.

The coroner counted 40 bullets
entering from the back
only one from the front.

The rookies fired the most rounds
masking their shaking fear.
the veterans fired stone cold and numb,
the wreckage of racism.
a mental disorder untouched by bourbon.

After the last news truck has gone
and the last hymn sung.
riding home quiet.

Remembering the words of the college acceptance letter
a deep grief pervades like oncoming fog
appearing and disappearing, chest pressing
leaving a soundless moan without air
of a gasping heart.

Days later, rising from her pew
rising from her voice
rising up
the enormous capacity for forgiveness
forged by history... an example for the world.

Love letter

my imagination was too small
the luminous circling universes
too few galaxies
and only a million "teeming with life" planets
not even a shoulder could fit through to another dimension!

imperfection dawns
with too much explaining
fussing over
mystical meanings with this little mind.

I will write myself a love letter
through the planes
leading home
home
forever and always
as you promised.

Toys ARE US!

consuming under a spell,
the money culture
kills hidden parts of the brain
that cannot be replaced,
the connective geometry fails, implodes on itself
resulting in limitation
stealing part of their nature.

in the store the harmful LED lights vibrate overhead with soft
dullness
the war toys are assaulting.
soldiers with advanced weapons.
the same guys as in the video game,
the landscape of armored vehicles, violent heroes, and pink dolls.

the spell drives on a cycle of throwaway garage sales,
back to the mall
buy another toy
after another
leaving the plastic
to real killing in the oceans.

Shamanic Work

now here come shapes
planet size,
perfectly void of dimension
                    no edge
                    no corner
                    no orbit.
they are filled with round music.
very few humans have heard this music
it is reserved for repairing bird wings and broken worlds.

don't be afraid
your wounds are
your story
your suffering
the entire illusion
dull like boiled water
is safe.

throw away your umbrella
this singing rain is always thirsty
falling for eons
filling in
where you are missing
the love song
of your Self.

Seppo Odell

Santa Fe

vibrations of this country
are bound in dirt
from below
where the
zuni
ancient memory bones lie,
carrying sadness for anything not loved.
soft wisdom soothing the badlands,
where human roots hold strong like sage in arroyos.

some that move here lose their weight
    they shed their arrogant skin
    they stop being busy
    they let go of the restless mind,
unlearn
and begin to remember their eternal drum song.

conditioned life peels away
like old yucca leaves
falling
crisp
beneath the starry new mexico night.

THE LONG MOMENT

Rushing
to move the caravan of love.
turning to hear a whisper,
"come here you are welcome"
Squeezed down and nourished
and grounded by earth
my hands clenched the red dirt of Central Park.

High above in the apartment
a loving guide-being watched from the corner,
silent hologram of light
I held on to the edge of the crib.
I saw them again but I think I was sixty.

*   *   *

My parents immigrated from Finland.
Mom from near the Russian border
strength like the backbone of a nation.
Dad from Helsinki
the son of a gangster and a good dancer.
they became servants
keeping the secrets of the rich.
we lived in the Bronx.
It took some time to learn english.
I understood people with the "immigrant's ear."
Grandma lived in Spanish Harlem,
we would go to the movies at 125th street.
Grandma was a cleaning woman
and vibrated like the planet saturn.
she would hang with mrs. Sepulveda on the stoop.
A white rose in spanish harlem.

*   *   *

Dad and I watched "Victory at Sea"
on our 17 inch black and white.
marching black waves

Seppo Odell

rising with the music
he tightened up compressed into his seat
sitting there like he was in the electric chair waiting for them
to throw the switch.
iwo jima flashes him back to the 4th division
filling the room with sulphur.
semper fi tattooed on his arm
training the corp in me
     of being on time, of brotherhood, of friendship
     of surviving anything
I remember his perfect hands
and invisible strength.

I spaced out with the idea of an Einstein, the bomb, and the
suffering of the Japanese people
so I washed the Chevy, the closest thing to driving.
leaving behind etheric planes and the thin air of imagination.
the Everly Brothers were soothing and so was Bela Lugosi.

I took the high school survival course for surviving high
school
where memorizing created more separation from your self.
History is now... oh wait now again... always now?
Then Catcher in the Rye and existentialism graduated me.

     *   *   *

There is a certain moan you can hear in the wind
filled with endless depth,
Allen Ginsburg reading"America" is a little like that
Sylvia P. James B. all the "beats" had that Miles Davis sad
introspective
stream lingering like blue cigarette smoke.
I left the moody BackBay bars and starched army jackets.

Sometimes a small act can stir this wind
like drinking from a fountain marked "whites only"
or sitting on a bus.
a Zion train was comin' at me!

marching with Dr. King
Howard Zinn
Noam Chomsky
the Boston cops club hard
my skin
knocked out reefer head
bleeding in the Boston Commons
For the first time
leaving the safety
of Ozzie and Harriet America.
Walter Cronkite never mentioned the cops.

dropped acid wearing Bob Dylan
on Beacon Hill,
with the garbage cans screaming at the street,
tripping out at medieval costumed weddings
as a past life actor.
with clean Osley acid
I watched my body
below on the couch… I'm not my body!
I watched my mind… I'm not my mind!
Who is watching?

          *   *   *

the Helsinki gypsies lived under the bridge:
fur hattted
hash boys
shared
brain freeze vodka,
they were like native people realizing their roots attached
to everything
they put me on the wrong bus
back to the University.

man's heart becomes hard away from nature.
organic mescaline in northern Germany
was not the vision quest I imagined
the army physical movie I starred in

Seppo Odell

holding my urine sample
like at a cocktail party
with my "johnny" on backwards
in the hearing test booth
trying to flunk the exam
I left them "Country Joe and the Fish"

comin' home after a long hitchhike
with a trucker who took too many uppers
he smoked some weed for the first time and calmed down.
we were the first long-haired hippies.
practicing effortlessly
beginners mind.

Alda's New Hampshire new poems,
reading in the firelight and unaffordable candles.
Robert Frost and Dylan Thomas good nights.
there is sex in some words.

the returning nam vet
walked into my apartment.
all my self-righteous shit melted
oh what a hurting heart
catatonic pain lay ahead
holding him with arms around
reading Tibetan text of the between.
the illusions of softer deaths
than the slaughtered children
we cry together for a long time.
he went away shouting
yelling at the gun factories Ike warned about
yelling at the phony priest
yelling until the orange chemicals return him to his cancer
coma.

whatever was me shattered
heart broken
I fell in love with the sufis!
real teachers appeared ... the spirit of guidance

the spirit of the dervish.
how to "see" like they see?
again, who is seeing?
I liked them
because they were always on the verge of being broke.

pizza with Ram Dass in Woodstock
all the eastcoast spiritual heavies were there
ram sita gurus came out to the streets.
the stoned mystic cowgirls drew me to the Mother,
opened Sita's breast in me,
opened the open secret.

the tribe breaks camp
we move from Woodstock to rural up-state
a community is formed
100 acres of Drama Yoga
and as we pushed and pulled against each other
a polishing was going on,
the true knowledge of being both within and without
emerged and 1000 centuries of karma
began to peel off while working in the garden
and nursing babies.
let it shine, let it shine.

Elijah the son-king opened the womb door
gifting lilas to a small family
eating the sea
a pirate and a master
playing at bedside.

The tribe grew organic grass
to soften
the chemotherapy/periwinkle flowers
taking my beloved through hell
she watched Magnum stoned
While I scrambled something for dinner.
A Pueblo medicine man
showed her the realms in the afterlife

of reading clouds.
my sweet wife awakened
aware of the perfect one
formless within
the Bardo of a thousand suns radiance!
her parents had never experienced such a funeral,
invoking all the masters, prophets, and saints
of all the religions that ever was or were or going to be.
no voids left unfilled or weak straws in the wind
parents grieving at dinner parties with too much wine.

an unknown family was found.
love on empty
with only pain in their pockets.
a love rocket
had locked on
a burning spear of new love
a warrior seer, oracle woman
a life guide.
she never ate left overs, and history was a waste of time.
in my bliss was included four children, a family dog, a station-
wagon, puberty, hormones, mowing the lawn!
The family crucible!
"t.s. eliot,
where is my freak flag?"

the luddite religious oligarchy ascends to power
new century america arrives with the perfect scenario
time for more war, more money.
minds mired in perpetual fear, separated by conflict.
ignoring the warm heart of the world
deepening its wound from Gaza to Manhattan,
so they strike the towers!
revenge culture takes off, masking the same greed
since Colombus.

      *   *   *

in the vastness
in Mayan time
galaxy alignments occur,
vibrating Gaia's core
creation raindrops turn into jungles.
the feminine goddess returns and turns
women towards their natural guidance system,
revealing the power of monthly blood.
their eyes see, seeing and men begin weeping

Earth is mother, ocean is mother
she allows her children to choose
here in the "free will" zone.
it is likely that women will save the world.

by grace
like Hafiz and Rumi
consciousness awakens to itself
knowing endless happiness
I eat the world!
as a condition
of divine satisfaction.

Seppo Odell

Amnesia

hidden
in last nights dreams,
fear slipped in,
disguised
as an event that took place yesterday morning
outside Starbucks
with a homeless person.
you don't remember,
it was about
getting money.
it was about how uncertain you have become,
giving away your power

you live with your sixty thousand daily thoughts
they are all unoriginal.
they are
sand piled on a beached winter fish.

You fill space with time
your kids
grow-up fast and busy
learning how to assert
how to use objects and people
how to wear your psyhic suit
and win at everything
all the while
taking away their childhood
their imagination
of the glorious possibilities
within the inner being of an evolving human.

You keep seeing the BLACK GODDESS,
She visits you in your dreams
She visits your friends and many others

you are afraid of her
she lives under the concrete …
and will burst through
during your daylight amnesia
telling you
to just STOP!

ANGELFIRE

down on the street far from the sharia,
a muslim cabby watches
a beautiful African Rasta woman ...
moving
clean
as a cat ...
crossing the street
whispering her song, "Jah no dead ... Jah no dead"
her presence melts him into a vulnerable mess
religion dissolves into warm kindness.

the cosmos giggles
as she confers her incomprehensible fire
  "stop all this killing ... in the name of the beloved Prophet,
                                he is not on the battlefield!
he is tending his flock ... protecting the fatherless ...
caressing the motherless."

down on the street   cruising drug free,
the guilty convict
converted pimp
         tunes
         his walkman to "Radio Rock Jesus"
 "the man is talkin' the christian news, the problems, the
queers, the hollywood jews, the ..."
Rasta woman rises-up hot
Her blood power ... singes
starting a fire!
his jeans tighten
pressure pressing skin
leaving behind the lonely life of hard secrets!
she whispers softly,
"sweetie, you are the secret of the meek ... fearless in your
perfection."

down on the street, the guru of spiritual knowledge arrives,
trading dreams of illumination for his disciples' stuff!
like a busy sniffing dog lookin' for bones
he makes his collection … his hidden scam
leaving the bewildered flock crushed
the painful truth of teachers
"you can learn from a bad teacher as long as you love them"

Rasta woman sighs
rolls her eyes.
Turns the guru into a woman
creating another dawn
her breath burns the concrete!
moving like a magic wind
to another street.

down on the street clutching his Haggadah.
a young man leaves the Seder early
his tight brain down
a complex of toxic thought- forms .
leaving behind the waiting for the next "the looming holocaust"
leaving the survivor-father of the new brother-in-law,
completing the family circle guy,
sitting at the table eating hard crumbs.
"It never stops!!
"I want a cheeseburger … a moment … not to be jewish."

he sees her,
"You are so beautiful! Who are you?"
Rasta woman smiles,
soothing
her easy fire eyes burn off his karmic stories about existence.
"I am both King and Queen of the Kosmos" she announces.
"now you are free of the stains of thousands of years."

Hunger at Whole Foods

no cardboard burgers
coca-cola chemistry
sugar sugar
fries!

subarus
fill the lot.
dread locked
patchouli oiled
children of solomon
smoke-up
an ancient
way
that is clean with love.

inside there is the running tension
of
flawless bodies and just regular ones,
rampant unconscious thought forms are released
collect in the corners
making it hard to move
the cashiers are waiting
wearing a nametag with their story
okay … okay

I have a hunger!
so exquisite
a burning storm
of dissolving rains
until i am absent
with no furniture in my rooms.

Memory Lane

the faces are frozen in the family photo album
the only animations
are my imaginations of their unspoken thoughts
like a whole world without wind.

I am the same actor in all the pictures
a moment of this life
the moment of feeling the emotions alive in colors
and talking to yellow.
or messages trapped in crystal geometrics
their secrets.
the vibes of vermont
the cows in new jersey.

as I turn the last page
I erase myself
allowing the speedy mind atoms to release their form
rising with no memory
turning into a very fine heavenly music!

I see below me the whirl of incessant thoughts
like the nervous scratching of chickens
beneath a calm elephant.

This is a very startling end to arrive at!
the limit and end of thinking
just spinning
where the mind cannot capture itself.

then all at once ... all-at-once hits
it just arrives ... is there before arriving!
awareness is always
out and out and further
without moving it is already arriving
the divine perfection at the rough edges of creation.

Seppo Odell

WOODPILE

before feeling
the smell
never seeing it begin arrives
without thought
the woodpile
has been
collecting
quiet
snow.

SUFI DANCING

the dance hall
decorated with
posters of stars
hangs in the sky
a new wind
a secret blowing
over the world.
children begin turning
whirling mature turns
smiling in the solar dust
the Creator's sweet story,
calling
to
dance
with wind movements branches sway
whispering the zikar.

THE BOXES

Now here come big boxes universe size,
perfectly void of dimension
        with no orbit.
        filled with round music
            that has no edge or corner.
 no human has heard this music.
 it is reserved for repairing butterfly wings and broken worlds.

Hush!
one of the lids is opening
upon hearing
some humans begin melting
losing their free will
having no shape as though they never were!

Don't be afraid
your wounds are safe!
if you want
your broken heart will come back.

Throw away your umbrella
this thirsty rain is always falling love drops
singing for you
so you can hear your own healing.

STUCK INSIDE THE WILLIAM BEN HOGAN HOTEL

Located in the middle of the city
for some time
then moved and moved again
(and had nothing to do with the famous golfer)
some smarty pants gave it that name just for fun.
the rooms were clean, plain, that's all.
no one really slept.
the atmosphere was a pervading sameness of everything
empty weight
everywhere
making shapes of energy
out of families grafted and stitched together
as they took in their first breaths of zyklon long ago.

at first i felt hollowed.
finally, "check out" came.
and they were gone
unstuck, freed toward the brightest light.
oh what joy!

Seppo Odell

NOTHING NEW UNDER THE SUN

republican democratic
supersize s.u.v.
soccer den mothers!
Your thoughts are safe with me
imagination is just too scary for you!

the wise Woman
the ancient eyes that guides men buried
somewhere in your house.
Isis hides
between the pages of Town & Country,
culture has halted
stopped!

you know everything is connected!
bad breathing air
bad mothers' milk
melting glaciers
dead forest
confused cells.

stir yourself up   pyramid Priestess!
awaken your sons!
so busy creating
more
greed culture
frat house beers
on the lawn
the date rape babes
graduating
asleep in the dorm
class after class
while the Earth turns into Mars.
Come on, Mom ...!

Two

matter
frozen in the world of twos.

the Creator weaves a miniature repeat pattern
the same oval
in the same color
over and over
inside the ten pointed star
where children repeat
dying young
in the wars of unevolved men.

For No Reason

grace showed up
unleashed
quickly
within
the steel mill heart
burning ribbons like white magnesium
taking
all the oxygen.

every love
every
falling in love
every
heartache
every pain.
all the broken longings,
making
another long night
the joy
of grateful
searing tears
never ends.

Air Bus

she cleaned
herself,
scrubbing twice
sensed her smell.
pulled tight her bun,
groomed
polished white
nutlet.

the long flight home
unknown lives
all around
surrounded with no room
who will sit beside me
too tight
in the air
the perfume of fear.

Seppo Odell

No Gas

birds land
singing
on a windy phone wire,
below
an old filling station.
clanging signs read
"closed."

except for swarms of old flies
in all the windows
soundless behind the glass
moving never resting.

with dusk wind
the birds fly off into the dark.
The flies stop
frozen
in the mercury lights
illuminating
the familiar culture
the eerie lonesome landscape
of rusting
cars.

Far Out Acid

the moon is always hidden
and knows no reason
for reason
from
deciding
what is for dinner!
no freak flag or peace tabs here
just
older hair
and
this blue thin
white moonlight
calming
the false struggle
of being
separate
from allness
and the old fears of having something to lose.

Seppo Odell

Blue Collar Buddha

The electrician's face
is grey
in
the winter windshield,
snowmelt grime
flying in the wheel wells
driving to the job at dawn
young and
numb.

our pick-ups meet
as though in slow motion,
his head turns to face me
I see him ... an ancient one!
rousing the bodhi heart
in an instant
our tires splash each other
my heart heaves
pierced
for miles down the road.

IRELAND

farmers lie in ancestral fields
dreaming in carrageen
hearing the deep song
burning within
thousand year peat.
above
the organic vegetables grow past their bloom
undisturbed
by strong sea wind.

a mother stands firm on the Sunday Road
wearing the necklace of mystic moons
blue and luminous
she guards the graveyards
that caress
the Meath
Brian Boru
the Pale left behind Poynings Law.

redhead fenian children
fearless with paint
draw emotions on walls
pictures of the cause
in the noonday sun
conceived at night with a drum
by errant Saints
mingling in the everyday life
of common suffering.
Irish dirt
under their fingernails
spawning
the earthbound magic
that stirs and
arouses the world.

Seppo Odell

ALDA

there is a stone
on your thigh
pocket
made smooth over years
of touching.

a black square flag
hangs
in your wind mind.
Uncontrolled
you illuminate
one side red.
as if seen for the first time.

"water or don't water the flowers
I don't care
they will bloom."
are you ready to hoist a new flag?
discover the grand
immense country
you live within
where flocks of white geese
fly overhead
across your clear skies

night is delicious
hot moonlight streams,
pours poetry
soft hands hold glasses
covering
your face
the complete
focus
of your smiling eyes.

Your sleigh glides easily
over the world's
snowless ground.

Seppo Odell

BEING IN LOVE

Being in love
is stillness
through luminous liquid blackness
without end,
where dreams and shoes are left at the door
conferring a kind of being
to my nearest friend

Dervish Chant

i am in deep waiting for you, standing
without ground nor feet
a naked alert planet
in a deers eye!
You leave clues in me
about our mystery.

FAINT SLEEP

save this dream
for me,
for I am absent
we are oldest lovers.
you   dearest friend
when you wanted to know yourself
as me   as a condition of you.

what is never absent
silently
records the merits of spiritual achievements,
but forget it
virtues dissolve ...
only satisfaction and your presence
matters.

North Shaman Sweat

sauna sweats are extreme, you can't tell if your
skin is boiling or freezing or of no temperature!

Unlike the ice powder snow covered chair,
steam rising from me sitting there
weightless spirit streams taking me to the sacred directions
the reindeer - west, wolf - south, eagle - east and bear - north.

Out of body
ungrounded in no space
to face the truth of my body planet
to sense the perfume of my exquisite fineness
to the radiance of heaven on fire
to the exaltation expanding like a gas mingling with all
exhalations.

Grounded
shaking back into the sweet moist birch heat
a deep primordial awareness of being human.

Seppo Odell

BIKERS

The great owl watches from his perch.
astonished,
"they look like large ants that live in old trees, but ride wheels!
their heads are pointy with colored tight skin
glistening in the sun.
they move together as though some prehistoric instinct pulls
them with purpose!"

We are all made of the same Stardust.
some of us share some of our parts with other parts of creation.
The great owl knows this along with all of Nature.

Science Fiction

the nirvana scientists
worry
that
nirvana may have to include diaper changing and vacuuming
"not in my nirvana!" they say.

we are all in Buddha's long range plans
reality will dawn upon us
blow apart everything unreasonable.
leaving us with the good sense
of never ending bliss

Seppo Odell

First Grade

the separation started
when first told to memorize
dullness
that was not linked to anything,
striking fear chords,
scenarios of limitation,
learning to only please
wearing the Sears
wool suit on Sunday,
clothed
because they were cold.

I now know
all the while
I was free
and
indivisible.

Soft Science

out of the solitude of unknowing,
intelligence plans itself as light,
            with no direction
            or sense of place   a stage is set.

silent portals open to a star traveler
drawn by love
propelled by their own current
nearing earth time begins to thicken space
            as the way water moves through ice.

earthbound the traveler drops
a gentle blue light
a balm of
bundled geometries
so the physics of a circle
can help a spiral understand itself,
can capture the moment of its joyful curving.

the star traveler understands earth,
earth as an old poem
read and re-read
treasures of memories
of souls who have read her lines,
evolving in unbounded bliss
loving the wonder of being solid.

Seppo Odell

DEER ASPIRIN

the corporate scientists
stalk the forest animals
recording what they eat
they are looking for a pain drug.

a delicate
soft southern light
between the yellow and blue spirits
removes the deer's pain.

the lab-men call out
the medicine-man from his trailer.
He smiles like a sun furnace,
the lab-men wait in rapt attention for his answer,
"the grass works," he says
"if you
  are in
  the consciousness of a deer,
  and you love the deer."

I Do Not See You

i do not see you
as the thought
you hold of yourself.
but as a cosmic learner.
an invisible vortex of stardust
      with million year skin
      as a soft toad
mutating into jaguar jungles
your tribe's pride.

a life spent in the roman army
     alert on guard
     reading clouds, trees, and ravens
     for hints of what is to come.

a wisdom woman weaving and dyeing wool
     with clear glacier water.
     dreaming in the solitude
     of emotional events on another world.
neck hairs stiffen
a breath blows behind me

the familiar awareness
that you are a treasure

Viet Nam

i saw you having dinner with your wife,
it was awkward for me.
the rippling patriarchy with each bite
drippings off your fork
staining the table cloth.

do you know who sits across from you?
how SHE has been waking up for centuries,
every day on the line
waiting the endless hours
holding place.
watching
killing soaking
earth with blood.

she allows you to do this
so you might evolve.
The Buddha Mother.

you've given your self to propaganda
you are unclear
chaos and fear
cowboys and indians
kimosabe's guns
cops and more cops.
betty crocker with her new appliances makes you cookies,
dad's pretty model who hides Her power!

i'm so sorry you killed so many
women
just fleeing you
and the senators that sent you
and their children ready to start another conquest.

the battle of YOU has just begun
how will you understand trees and rocks again?
boyhood will not help you,
or drugged catatonic dreams.

go home as intimate human
find feeling
go softly surrendered
she is your wounded healer
she has opened her throat
to speak truth to you
like a planet.

i love the core of you
i cry deeply in the vast inside
of you and me.

Seppo Odell

1987

quantum gravity
stirred,
failed,
settled into a rare stillness
waited
for the poles to shift.

fast gold streams
of alien seeds
shot at earths geometric lines
carrying new DNA codes
that will be used
for the collective
unprocessed
fear
of cataclysms
and the glorious birth
that will follow.

Sphere of Influence

it appears   then disappears
roundness with opaque colorlessness
then hues of color like a soap bubble
not really third dimension
not the "counting" mind
not time or space
not arriving then staying behind
the sphere is enormous and small
inside me outside me
the pure clean serene presence
the emotion of longing disappears
even the sphere goes away
leaving a residue
of the intelligence
of yielding to the flow of life.

HAFIZ

newly lost love pierces
like ice
the clean way
a wound
sucks in
the cold
moonlight air
alone with
no one waiting for you.

make this pain your very best friend!
fresh sorrow is just a door   slightly ajar...
push it ... go in.
this is the most important work for humans
their separation from the beloved.

RED CHI BIRD

there is only one red chi bird on the earth.
the rest move in small angry groups
pecking
managing
wearing down resistance
flitting in the dark
   looking for the illusive red movement,
   in trees, grasses and swamps,
   watching the city
unaware that they are color blind
dull and oily.

red chi bird lands on a summer beach
   a young girl
   forming new breasts
   giggles at the thought
   of being seen
   in the fall in the hall
   of the high school.
   red chi bird smiles at nature's clock.
flying high
seeing over her red wing
a family
mom looking for lost sand toys,
   on the shoreline her babies crawl
   fully dilated in the wet ecstasy
   upon hearing the red chi bird.

"Where is dad? Where is dad?"
practicing his swing
making deals in the clubhouse
  destroying countries
  selling his cheap stuff
  their reward for being defenseless.

Seppo Odell

Red chi bird's mission
spans the world healing the disfigured orphans from wars.
guiding the changing migrations
in the new climate.

Red chi bird bows to the Mother,
whose water gets very liquid
when the waves pray
each one aware they are the whole ocean.

MARTY

Earth fires
burn
deeply
beneath heavy wet grass
softened by gold green light
in the jade chinese coin earrings you wear,
dangling as if in slow motion
as you move in the world,
carrying rich secrets,
never repeating your answers.
blessings of sounds a wise voice
makes
like the hum of eternal bees.

Seppo Odell

UPON THE POPE'S RESIGNATION

the thirteenth imam is absent,
he is with the Buddha.
he has been gone since the last Goddess ruled over the
earth.
he will call up Abraham, Isaac, and Sulemon
they will break the illusions of sinless suicide bombers,
who think they skip judgement day.
he will guide the children on the bombed bus who will skip
a life.

who can you kill   Shalomites?
where is the calm heart of Islam?

The imam will be spellbound by Christ,
sweating blood in the garden
teaching to not resist evil
and children
in the mysterious presence of Mary.

the Seal of the Prophets has been off planet
now landed in Tibet.
he drones mantra of the afterlife
     how rivers of honey
     raging fires …
     the unconscious mind world
     are brought here
     with no guarantee of Paradise.
everyone goes to the transit lounge to wait.

the imam is happy singing … calling souls not yet born,
the poles sit
smiling on the smiling wall,
waiting

for the mercy that
quickens the earth's
links to the Messengers
waiting their turn
serving
on other worlds.

Seppo Odell

WARNING

through the window
fast wind clouds
form angry dragons.
the television in the next room
sounds like muffled
soft
distant thunder.
something about "national security."
a storm is coming
with
increasing pressure.

IN YOUR ARMS

in your arms
i die daily
a perfect
loose
thread
you unravel.
ripping veils
bending space
with riots
of shocking
light.
this is what it is like
to be your friend!
eating the world
in love.

Seppo Odell

THE NATIVE WAY

she felt it ... right away
read the message in the clouds.
turbulence rocked
dropped the 747.
the flight attendant's
necklace
grandmother made
tight to her throat
the great spirit's restful design
vibrates with yellow frequencies,
blanketing the passengers
calming their angst.

LIMINAL SPACE

The smell of rust
in the land
way after
the practical cows
formed a country with thoughts for everything
all the while
devas disguised as five year olds
keep calm
maintaining
simplicity
so mountains
keep their minerals
far from the factory.

Motherless

there is an eerie quiet in grief:
you only hear the edge of what is spoken to you.
it is as though you held your breath
in the unending absence.

the ordinary routines go on ... I take you to school.
I take myself to work ... I feed us.
we look outside
and above the same sky ... and then imagine of the space
beyond.

we now have an understanding we never had before
I wonder if you know it
maybe in fetal sleep.
we are launched once again into a life that seems new.

the caravan of love has not abandoned us!
and when you finally exhale
I will drink wine and rejoice
with all the camel masters.

MOUNTAIN LIGHT

miles above the sea
full star night
presses down
cold space
pushing plinth bound pines.
branches
brushing
the cabin logs.
inside
a hot
brief
kiss goodnight
the promise of warm sleep.

Seppo Odell

ELIJAH VILAYAT

magic
night
a chameleon in the parlor,
draw back
the deep maroon
fat curtains.
unseen
hiding in the folds
an old setting moon
from centuries
before.

dawn
at the shore
reveals
five perfect mounds
of white sand
untouched
by wind
or waves.
the work of a little boy
the day
before.

Mineral War

how do I weave your
combat life
into words,
shuffled around
like this war
imploding
feelings
deeper than crying.

you could not imagine dying this month
a month, too far away
but today, in the next minute!
you smoke one after another
on guard under a dome of dust
brain pushed in tired
waiting
for the fear of objects
to subside.

then there is the guy
who sent that hapless drone
killing the wrong family
of the guy
who blew himself up murdering your buddies.
the drone tech
goes to therapy,
goes home,
plays basketball with his kids,
on a clean driveway in Maryland

part two

on duty in a black moonless night
delicious

like back home in west texas
and the crazy one the villagers call madzub
his twinkling santa claus eyes
spoke to you,
"your wounds have not healed
the deeper ones lie below the sun
in another dimension."
the magic lapis desert
with wind sounds speaking
through earth's geometrics
dissolves
the tapes running around in your head.
in deep dreaming
you step into the thin air of eternity
cleaned and healed
where no therapist could reach
what luck!

GAIA

There is nothing wrong with planet earth.
the science doctors report her failings,
the evening news shows her in peril,
        an entertaining drama of dark funnel clouds!
these are distractions that form attractions
to automobiles, devices, and glamor
noisy meaningless plastic phantom things!

Go to her with the glad heart of a child,
her mind is space itself
she will not refuse you
abandon you
any longer than any measure of time.

Seppo Odell

REALIZATION

i am the present day Buddha
the second coming of Christ
the fulfillment of Mohammed's teaching.
Black Elk's echo.
the reincarnation of Persian poets.
how could I not be?
the lover like a veil
covering
the nameless one calling
longing to know its self
in complete satisfaction
as the only perfect being
if ever there was a being
the only one
and yet this is but a slight blush on the Mother's cheek.

Beach Sand

dry tomato seeds stuck
between poetry pages...
a hapless summers'
white mushy bread
with mayo.
a stained reminder of words
written in the sand wind
pushing all around the beach.
hearing the voice in the moving grains
praying in the water for no reason.
knowing happiness
is the slant of wind
where i sail
where i have always been
savant of the quiet hallelujah.

Seppo Odell

CODA

at the coarse edges of creation
fire turns to light
emotions spill out with ardor.

elegant humans write about themselves on sunwarm
primordial rocks.
scratching warning symbols
translating their star wisdom
so others who come after them,
would know, especially their arrival long ago.

They also write of a feeling place
of being there
unseen without form,
dissolving the illusion of being separate from anything
they called it "a knowing"
and then sometimes simply
the silent thin reach between souls.

GOLD RIVER WOMAN

from a distance
out of the sea's horizon
a woman emerges on a horse,
adorned with rich colored bands
streaming in gold sunlight.
her crystal jewels
creating prisms
making small fires
sparks in the air.

she performs a majestic ritual to the sun,
for the ascent of her children
dramatizing the mystery of light.
they splash in the receding tide,
while she feeds them
with the unending
flow of love.

Seppo Odell

ORDINARY ENLIGHTENMENT

Afterwards you are the same.
free from delusion
no matter how nice   how beautiful   how ugly.
as if you have misspelled a word since grammar school
                  and the correct spelling dawns upon you.
with little notice of illusions
you drop some things   needing less force on things.
you change reality   looking at it head on
and get out of the way
with everyday mind or
shaman sage wise mind
no matter it is the same mind.
it is like when it rains
water falls on everything.

INDEX OF POEMS

Seppo Odell

About the Author

A poet, mystic and astrological consultant, Seppo Odell has been at the forefront of Western explorations in consciousness and awakening during much of his adult life.

Born in New York City after his parents immigrated from Finland, he graduated Boston's Suffolk University, then went to Helsinki for graduate studies. He soon realized the academic path was not for him.

He studied mysticism, and took initiation in a Sufi Order in 1972, where he met extraordinary beings including Shamcher Beorse, Pir Vilayat Inayat Khan, and connected with Murshid Samuel Lewis through his immediate students. Working as a carpenter with conscious awareness has expanded and sustained him throughout the decades.

A mentor and inspirational guide, Seppo currently lives in Colorado with his wife Marty, and their Labrador, Lilly.

More info at www.odell.shamcher.com

What did Rudolph's girlfriend say to him?
You brighten my day.

What did Rudolph say to his girlfriend when
he picked her up for their date?
You look nice, deer.

What did the boy kitty cat say to his girlfriend? You're purrrrrrr dee.

Why don't clams and oysters share their dinners? They're two, shell fish.

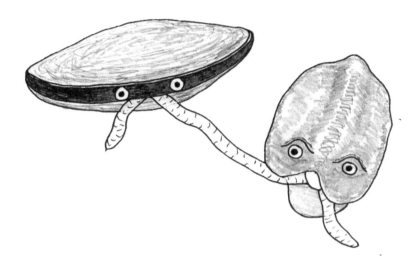

How do you pay a dollar to get into a basketball game, watch the whole game, and then get your money back? When you watch the whole basketball game you get four quarters.

**Why did the man in jail want to catch the measles?
Because, he wanted to break out.**

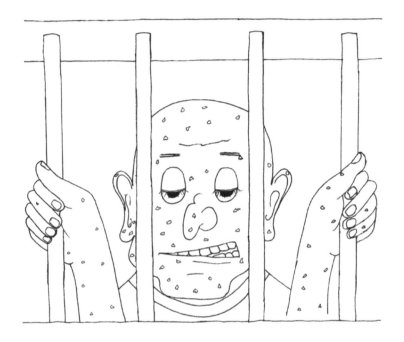

**Where did Egyptian mummies store
their automobiles?
In their funny car-tombs.**

A chicken feed salesman was going from farm to farm, and one chicken decided to buy her own chicken feed, so how much did it cost her? Three baucks, "Bauck, bauck, bauck."

If you're in the woods and you pick up a bunny, why should you try not to get scratched? Because you don't want a hare cut.

A man noticed a germ on his hand, and the germ started talking, the man did not understand one word, so he asked the germ " what language are you speaking?"
The germ said, "Germ-man."

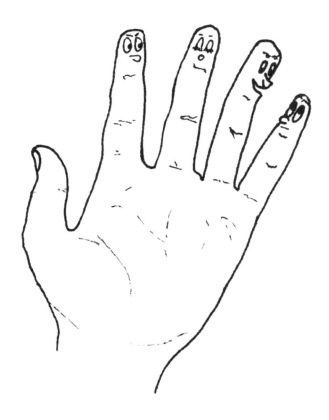

What did one finger say to the other finger?
People count on me.

Why was everyone afraid to go to the restaurant
on Halloween night? Because the restaurant
only served sand-witches, and
had a skeleton crew.

Why was the skeleton toddler afraid to
go to the bar-b-q pit restaurant?
Because he heard the most popular
meal was baby- back ribs.

Why did Barbie scream when the waitress spilled bar-b-q sauce on her? Because she did not want to be Bar-bie-cu'ed.

What drink does a boxer try to avoid?
Punch

If a nut has a silly friend what would he be called?
A nutty buddy.

**What do you get when you cross a dog
with a cow?
A bow - wow - cow.**

**Why do many people think snowmen are
unfriendly? Because many people get a cold
shoulder from snowmen.**

**When a snowman is sick, what does
he usually have?
A head cold.**

What did the debt collector say to the duck?
You have a large bill.

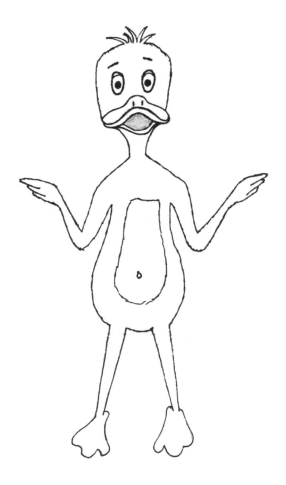

What did the tow truck driver say when he went
to Wing Fu's Chinese restaurant to pick up
Wing's car? Tow fu?

When the kids came back to the room after recess, they saw Jimmy looking into the mirror. They said, "Jimmy, why are you staring into the mirror? He said, " Before recess I said something I should not have said, and the teacher told me to watch my mouth."

Why did one corn salute the other corn?
Because the other corn was a kernel.

Why did the ghost go to the doctor?
Because he had a boo-boo.

What do you call a parent who helps with the
school band? A band – aide.

What did the fish say to the talkative oyster?
Clam up!

**Why did the sky think she should see a
psychiatrist?
Because she was feeling blue.**

**Why did the toast stay out of the sun?
Because it was already too dark.**

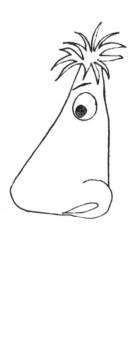

**What did the nose say to the little girl when she
made fun of the nose? That snot funny.**

The grandmother hugged her little grandson and said, "You're getting so big! I bet you've grown another foot."
The little boy looked down and said, "No grandmother, I still have only two feet."

Why did the frog go to the doctor?
Because he was afraid he might croak.

What does a frog do when his car won't start?
He asks his friend for a jump-start.

**What does a monster do when he gets a
sore throat? He gargoyles!**

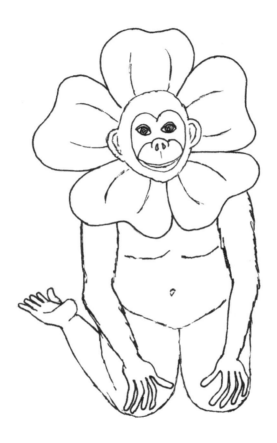

**What flower only grows in the zoo?
The chimp - pansy.**

**What shoe is not a good gift giver?
The one with strings attached.**

What did the heart patient say when he was
revived by the doctors? I'm shocked!

What was Mr. Mouse's window cleaning
business' slogan?
We have a squeaky clean reputation.

Why did the fireman put the dog out?
Because the fire would have made him a hotdog.

**Why did the chicken fail her social studies test?
She was just a dumb cluck.**

**Why did little the piggy never want to go to the
beach on a hot sunny day?   Because he
didn't want to be bacon in the sun.**

**What do you call a crazy person from Brazil?
A Brazil nut.**

**Which shoe has a nickname and would be right
at home in prison? Lefty**

**Why did the lady think the kitty cat that had no
money, could swim? Because she thought it was
a poor-puss.**

**What did the little girl yell when she threw
her watch off the empire state building?
Watch out!**

**What do geeky California spiders like to do?
Surf the web.**